BEYOND MARKS AND MISTAKES

THE CLASSROOM OF LIFE

(Moral Stories)

Beyond Marks and Mistakes The Classroom of Life

by

Neethu U.V.

First Edition	: May 2025
Prepress Work	: Book Nest Publishing
Press Work	: Repro India Ltd
Distribution Partner	: Repro India Ltd
Cover Design	: Sujith R.S.
Published by	: Book Nest Publishing
Phone	: +91 94966 49547 | +91 96561 61635
Email	: booknestpub@gmail.com
ISBN	: 978-93-49488-29-8

For permissions and inquiries, contact:
Book Nest Publishing
Phone : +91 97785 80700
Email : booknestpub@gmail.com

ISBN 9789349488298

9 789349 488298

Price : ₹160.00

BEYOND MARKS AND MISTAKES

THE CLASSROOM OF LIFE

NEETHU U.V.

BOOK NEST PUBLISHING
THIRUVANANTHAPURAM

Neethu U.V.

Native of Venganoor, Thiruvananthapuram. Currently pursuing the first year of B.Ed. at Government College of Teacher Education.

Educational Background

- Primary education at Badlehem Primary School, Government L.P.S. Muttakkad, and Government L.P.S. Mudippuranada.
- High school and higher secondary education at Venganoor Girls Higher Secondary School.
- Completed C.A. Foundation and Intermediate studies at ICAI Chapter, Thiruvananthapuram.
- M.Com. from Kerala University, Karyavattom Campus.

Literary Contributions

Short stories and articles have been published in renowned publications such as Mathrubhumi, Sahithya Chakravalam (the official journal of Kerala Sahitya Akademy), Metro Manorama, Manorama News, Akshara Kairali, Sahitya Sahakarana Sangham, Kala Kaumudi, Kesari, and various other platforms.

Published Works

- Chandratheeram (Novel) – 2015
- Garalangana (Novel) – 2018
- Vifalamiyaathra (Poetry Collection) – 2021
- Varathetakal (Short Story Collection) – 2022
- Usha (Short Story Collection) 2025
- GST Prospects and Challenges: A Data-Driven Analysis
- Economic Disparity and Gender Equality (Published in Akshara Kairali Magazine – Kerala Department of Culture) Volume 11, December 2023
- Innovate to Elevate: The Entrepreneur's Guide to Thinking Beyond Limits (Kindle)
- The heart of teaching: lessons that last a lifetime (Kindle)
- Jaakko Hintikka: Revolutionizing The Philosophy Of Knowledge

Email: neethuuv2000@gmail.com

Publisher's Note

At Book Nest Publishing, we have always believed that the power of storytelling lies not just in entertainment, but in the ability to touch hearts, inspire minds, and transform lives. Beyond Marks and Mistakes: The Classroom of Life by Neethu U.V. is a shining example of this belief, bringing forth a collection of stories that delve into the real essence of learning beyond textbooks and academic achievements.

This book is more than just a compilation of moral tales; it is a reflection on the quiet, everyday lessons that shape character and nurture empathy. Through relatable narratives, Neethu U.V. beautifully captures the struggles, dreams, and triumphs of young minds as they navigate the challenges of growing up. Each story not only entertains but also leaves the reader with a profound insight into the importance of kindness, perseverance, and the courage to learn from mistakes.

The stories presented here echo the values that every child, student, teacher, and parent can relate to. From embracing failures to understanding the true meaning of success, the pages of this book carry a message that resonates far beyond the classroom. In a world that often measures worth through marks and grades, this book gently reminds us that life's most valuable lessons come from experiences and the spirit of never giving up.

As publishers, it brings us immense joy to present Beyond Marks and Mistakes: The Classroom of Life to readers of all ages. We hope that this book will inspire a deeper understanding of the journey of learning, where both achievements and mistakes are part of a larger, beautiful story.

We sincerely thank Neethu U.V. for sharing her thoughtful vision through these stories, and we hope that this book becomes a source of motivation, guidance, and reflection for its readers.

Warm regards,

Book Nest Publishing

Dedication
To my parents —
my roots, my wings.

Before the Bell Rings

"Beyond Marks and Mistakes: The Classroom of Life" is more than a collection of experiences—it is a journey through the quiet, unseen lessons that life teaches beyond the pages of any textbook. These reflections capture the wisdom life has gently offered me through moments, people, and the world around me.

It is often difficult to see the light when surrounded by shadows. Yet, I have always chosen to seek out the positive—not only in my own life but in the lives of those who are less fortunate. I have found meaning in standing with them, learning from them, and growing through them. This book is my humble attempt to bring those silent stories to light—the ones that shaped me and whispered truths that no classroom ever taught.

As I pen these thoughts, I carry in my heart both the people who lifted me and those who doubted me. Their presence—whether in support or resistance—has shaped my path. To those who encouraged me to write, and even to those who tried to stop me, I owe the strength that led to this book. Every obstacle became a lesson. Every silence, a story.

I invite you to walk with me through these reflections. Perhaps, somewhere in these pages, you may find a piece of your own story too.

With gratitude,

Neethu U.V.

Table of Contents

The Day Natasha Learned to Love

"Too often we underestimate the power of a touch, a smile, a kind word, a listening ear, an honest compliment, or the smallest act of caring — all of which have the potential to turn a life around."

— Leo Buscaglia

In a peaceful little village surrounded by green hills and swaying trees, lived a twelve-year-old girl named Natasha. She was intelligent, full of potential, and quick to learn. But despite her brilliance, there was something missing in her — the warmth of love and respect for others.

Natasha often acted stubbornly. She never listened to her parents or teachers. She did only what she pleased, without caring about the feelings of those around her. Every morning, she would lazily wake up and demand coffee from her mother as if it were her right. And if her parents or teachers tried to correct her behavior, she would throw a tantrum, sometimes even refusing to eat for the whole day. Her parents were heartbroken. They loved her dearly but were deeply worried about her cold attitude and unhealthy behavior.

One day, during school hours, Natasha was playing in the playground. In her excitement, she tripped and fell hard on the ground, scraping her leg badly. Blood started oozing out, and she began to cry out in pain.

Hearing her cries, her classmates and teachers rushed to her side. They surrounded her with concern and care, trying to soothe her.

One of her friends gently held her hand and whispered, "Don't worry, you'll get better soon."

Tears welled up in her classmates' eyes seeing Natasha in pain. Her teachers immediately took action. They carried her to the nearest hospital and informed her father about the accident. Within minutes, her father arrived at the hospital, worry etched deep on his face.

When he saw Natasha crying uncontrollably despite the wound being minor, his heart broke. He rushed to her side, knelt down, and gently held her hand.

"My dear daughter," he said softly, "it will heal soon. Don't cry. We are all here with you."

But Natasha wouldn't stop crying. Her sobs only grew louder. Her father looked at her closely, sensing something deeper was troubling her.

"What's wrong, my dear?" he asked gently. "I know you're strong. This little wound wouldn't make you cry so much. Tell me, what's really hurting you?"

Natasha looked up at her father, then at her teachers who stood nearby. Her lips quivered as she tried to speak, and finally, with a small, shaky voice, she said, "I'm sorry, Papa."

Her father was taken aback. "Sorry? For what, dear?"

She turned toward her teachers, tears streaming down her face.

"I'm sorry, teachers. I thought you didn't care about me. I never listened to you or respected you. But when I was hurt, you were the first to come running. You took care of me like your own child. My friends stood by me and comforted me. I was wrong all along. From today, I promise to be obedient. I love you all."

Her father's eyes brimmed with tears. For years, he and her mother had prayed for a moment like this — a moment when Natasha would finally open her heart. He embraced her tightly, and the teachers too leaned in, holding her close with love and affection.

From that day on, Natasha's life changed. She became a loving and kind-hearted girl, respectful toward her parents, obedient to her teachers, and caring toward her friends. She discovered the beauty of giving and receiving love, and she enjoyed the peace and happiness that came with it.

Moral of the story:

Value those who genuinely care for you, and respond with respect and kindness. A heart filled with love not only brightens the lives of others but also fills your own life with happiness.

The Spark Beyond the Comfort Zone

"Life begins at the end of your comfort zone."
— Neale Donald Walsch

In a bustling city lived a teenage boy named Adam with his loving parents, Ram and Rajni. Adam was a kind-hearted child, well-mannered and obedient. His parents adored him, pampered him, and made sure he never had to face any hardships. He grew up in a protective bubble where every need was met before he even asked.

Adam had dreams—big dreams. He wanted to become a successful business entrepreneur, to build something of his own and make a mark on the world. But there was a catch. He didn't know how to begin, and worse, he had never taken a decision on his own. He lived too comfortably, too safely, always within his little cocoon.

One evening, as his father returned from work, Adam approached him with a concerned look.

"Father," he asked softly, "what should I do to become a great entrepreneur?"

Ram smiled, appreciating his son's curiosity. He placed a gentle hand on Adam's shoulder.

"My dear son, dreams are beautiful. But to make them real, you need effort—persistent and passionate effort. You must work tirelessly and be ready to face failures too."

Adam nodded, trying to absorb his father's words. Yet deep inside, he still felt lost. What kind of effort? How much? Where should I begin?

That summer, Adam's family visited his grandfather's home in a peaceful village. The simplicity of rural life was new to him. But the best part was spending time with his grandfather, a wise and retired headmaster who had a lifetime of stories to share.

One sunny morning, while sitting on the veranda sipping tea with his grandfather, Adam opened up.

"Grandpa," he said, "I want to become an entrepreneur. But I don't know how. I want to succeed, but I'm afraid to take risks."

His grandfather chuckled warmly.

"You're fourteen now, right?"

Adam nodded, "Yes, Grandpa."

"When I was your age, I had to study and work just to buy bread for the day. You are lucky, you only study, and your parents take care of the rest."

"I know Grandpa," Adam said quietly.

"Child, what I'm trying to tell you is that comfort is good, but only to a point. If you never struggle, you may never realize the value of what you earn. You can't wait for others to push you forever. If you want to succeed, you must take risks. That's how you grow."

Adam's eyes lit up. "So, I have to take risks?"

"Yes, but smart ones," Grandpa smiled. "Come, I'll show you something."

He led Adam to the edge of the village where a massive iron factory stood. Machines roared inside, and smoke puffed from chimneys. The nameboard read: 'ABU IRON INDUSTRIES'.

"Do you know the story of this factory?" Grandpa asked.

Adam shook his head.

His grandfather began:

"Years ago, this entire land was just a dream in the eyes of a young man named Abu. He was a blacksmith, poor and struggling. He had to support his aging parents and two siblings. Life was not kind to him. Yet he dreamed of owning an iron factory."

Adam listened intently.

"But dreams don't come easy. Abu didn't have a single rupee to start. So he thought of pledging his small house—their only shelter—to raise money. It was a terrifying decision. If he failed, they'd have nowhere to live. But he believed in himself. His parents, too, trusted his dedication and gave their consent."

"So he took the risk?" Adam asked.

"Yes, he did. He pledged the house and started the factory. But the road wasn't easy. People laughed at him, mocked

ABU IRON
INDUSTRIES

him, said it wasn't his cup of tea. But Abu didn't respond with words. He responded with hard work. He worked day and night, never letting failures pull him down. Slowly, his business grew. And one day, those same people came back—not to mock, but to apologize and admire his success."

"Wow!" Adam's eyes widened.

"Abu didn't stop there. He began employing hundreds of villagers, expanded globally, kept learning, and helped those in need. He became more than just a businessman—he became a role model."

Grandfather placed his hand over Adam's.

"Success doesn't come wrapped in safety, my child. You must step out, take wise risks, and never stop learning. Now tell me, have you understood the real way to grow?"

"Yes, Grandpa!" Adam said with a new spark in his eyes. "I need to take smart risks and work hard with consistency!"

From that day onward, Adam slowly began making small decisions for himself. He faced challenges with courage, learned from every mistake, and treated people kindly. The boy who once lived in comfort began to live with purpose. And with time, he too carved his path to success.

Moral of the story:

Dreams alone won't lead you to success. Step out of your comfort zone, take risks, stay consistent, and work hard. Only then can you truly grow and achieve greatness.

Beyond the Shadows: Seetha's Journey to Light

The fiercest light is born from the deepest shadow—and no hand can claim your flame but your own.

—Aisha Rahman

Seetha was a passionate and determined young adult, full of dreams bigger than her modest world. Her family lived a simple life—her father, a calm man with calloused hands, her mother, A soft-spoken woman who devoted herself to caring for her family and supporting them in every possible way. And her elder sister, a quiet presence with dreams of her own.

Seetha, however, carried a fire within. She dreamt of becoming a lecturer, an author, and an entrepreneur. She wanted to be someone who could inspire lives—not through noise, but through her words. During her teenage years, she wrote poems and stories that earned the admiration of her teachers. One such teacher was Mr. Manoj, an experienced figure in literature and teaching.

At the age of 13, Mr. Manoj noticed Seetha's talent.

"You write like someone who has seen the world through the eyes of wisdom," he told her during a school exhibition.

With her family's consent, he arranged for her first book to be published through a publisher —a proud moment for the young girl. He encouraged her, introduced her to literary groups, and inspired her to believe that greatness was within reach.

But as the years passed, something changed.

Mr. Manoj's guidance slowly turned into control. He began interfering with Seetha's personal decisions, her academic choices, and even her dreams. Whenever she spoke of starting her own publishing house, he would laugh it off.

"Do you know how much it costs to run a publication, Seetha?" he said once, half-mocking. "This isn't a child's game."

Everyone around her echoed the same sentiment. But her dream never faded.

Years passed. Seetha, now in her early twenties, had studied the nuances of publishing, saved every rupee she could, and finally took a leap of faith. She started her own publication. With sleepless nights and relentless effort, she published a book under her own banner.

When she shared the news with Mr. Manoj, he dismissed it again. "One book doesn't make you a publisher," he scoffed.

But Seetha stood her ground. "It's not about how many books. It's about courage," she replied, looking him in the eye.

He didn't respond. Instead, he began taking more interest in her venture—too much interest. Eventually, he proposed a partnership, which Seetha accepted, not seeing the hidden intent behind his friendly demeanor.

Three years passed. The business grew, but so did Mr. Manoj's interference. He discouraged her from taking new opportunities and even spoke to her parents.

"She should not divert her focus," he said calmly, but firmly. "She has potential here."

Her parents, though respectful, didn't give in. "It's her life. Let her decide," her mother said.

Soon, he tried to trap her with guilt and financial temptations.

"I'll pay you more than what that new opportunity offers," he said one evening.

"I never did this for money," Seetha replied, her voice steady. "You taught me that once."

He didn't stop there. He began manipulating people around her, spreading rumors, tarnishing her reputation.

One day, he came to her college.

"I need to make a call. My phone's dead," he said, with a friendly smile.

Seetha dialed the number and handed him her phone, not suspecting anything.

As soon as he took it, he turned cold.

"If you want this back, you need to stay in the publication," he whispered.

Seetha froze. Then, with a trembling but firm voice, she said, "Because of your control, I already left something I built with my heart. Please don't ruin me any further."

He didn't return the phone.

She didn't speak about the incident to anyone. Not out of fear, but because she didn't want her family to carry her burden.

But his behavior continued to grow more toxic. Even after her parents asked him to stop, he defied them. He tried to emotionally destroy her by turning people against her.

Finally, Seetha reached her breaking point.

With unwavering determination, she walked into the police station and filed a complaint. There, a woman approached her quietly.

"You're not alone," the woman said. "He misbehaved with me. I thought no one would believe me."

The truth hit Seetha hard. Until that moment, she had never thought he was deliberately harming women's lives. But now, she saw the full picture. He wasn't just controlling—he was dangerous.

With her complaint and the woman's testimony, Mr. Manoj was finally held accountable. The interference ended. The darkness lifted.

Seetha didn't stop. She worked silently, letting her actions speak. Even when people whispered about her, she never looked back. She knew her worth.

SEETHA PUBLISHING
BEYOND THE SHADOWS

A year and a half later, she launched a brand-new publication. The previous one, still in Mr. Manoj's hands, remained behind her—like an old chapter she had outgrown.

She never tried to ruin him, even after all he had done. That was not her way. Her strength came from walking forward, not turning back.

Moral of the story:

Never allow negative people to shape your destiny. Stay true to your dreams, and keep your circle filled with people who lift you up. The world may doubt your fire, but never let it extinguish. Your journey is yours alone—and it is worth every fight.

The Weight of False Words

A single lie may win applause, but only truth earns trust—and without trust, we are truly alone.

— Meera Krishnamurthy

Navaneet was a 14-year-old boy who lived in a busy urban neighbourhood. He was privileged in many ways. His father served in the Army, and his mother worked as a government employee. But despite having a good life, Navaneet had a bad habit—he never spoke the truth.

He exaggerated everything. At school, he would make up stories about his achievements, his family, and even about things that never happened. His friends initially found him interesting, but soon, they began doubting him.

Whenever his father returned home on leave, Navaneet would boast to his friends, "My dad fought a battle at the border last month! He even defeated enemy troops!"

The boys were amazed.

"Really?" one of them asked.

"Yes! He's a real hero," Navaneet claimed with pride.

But his friends started sharing these stories with their parents. Slowly, the truth came out. The parents knew that Navaneet's father was a lower-ranked employee in the Army who worked in administration, not on the battlefield. They realized Navaneet was lying.

Word got back to his father.

One evening, his father sat Navaneet down and said sternly, "Why do you lie so much, son? Do you think this will make people respect you more?"

Navaneet lowered his head, "I... I just wanted them to like me."

His father, furious, raised his voice, "Respect doesn't come from lies. You're damaging your own name and others' trust. Don't ever lie again!"

He even slapped Navaneet out of anger and disappointment.

But Navaneet didn't change. He kept lying.

One night, his mother noticed him unusually quiet at the dinner table.

"Navaneet," she said gently, "Can I tell you a story tonight?"

Navaneet nodded.

His mother began, "Once in a kingdom far away, there lived a lyricist. As a child, he always made up stories and spoke false things about people. No one corrected him. Over time, lying became a habit—like breathing. He couldn't stop."

She continued, "When he grew older, he became a well-known poet in the king's court. People believed his words. The King admired him deeply."

Navaneet listened closely.

"One day, the lyricist spread lies about the King's wife, saying she was disloyal. The King, who trusted the poet blindly, started doubting his queen. He even punished some of his loyal servants based on the lyricist's false stories. The palace, once full of happiness, became cold and distant."

"What happened then?" Navaneet asked, eyes wide.

"The truth eventually came out," his mother said. "The King discovered that the lyricist was lying all along—not just about his wife, but about many people. Enraged, the King banished him from the kingdom. Years later, the lyricist lived alone, filled with regret. He had lost everything—his respect, his peace, his people—all because of his lies."

Navaneet's eyes filled with tears.

"Mom," he whispered, "Do people see me the same way? Like a liar no one can trust?"

His mother gently held his hand. "People may forgive mistakes made in ignorance, Navaneet. But if you knowingly hurt others with lies, yes, people will see you that way. More importantly, you'll begin to lose yourself."

"What should I do now?" he asked, his voice trembling.

"Stop lying. Speak the truth, even when it's hard. Make others happy with kindness, not false praise. Only then will peace come into your heart."

"Will God punish me for what I've done?" Navaneet asked softly.

His mother replied, "If you knowingly continue to lie, then yes, God will take note. But if you realize your mistake and choose to change, He will surely forgive you."

Navaneet hugged his mother tightly. "I promise, Mom. I won't lie again. I'll become better."

His mother smiled, her eyes filled with hope. "That's all I ask for."

From that day onward, Navaneet changed. He stopped making up stories and began living honestly. Slowly, people started trusting him again. He found true happiness—not in fake stories, but in real relationships built on truth.

Moral of the story:

Your words have the power to build or break. Don't ruin others with lies. Speak the truth, for false words may bring momentary pride, but truth brings lifelong peace. Karma always watches.

Today is Yours

Do not wait; the time will never be 'just right.' Start where you stand...

— Napoleon Hill

Anjaly and Aparna were twin sisters, alike in appearance but vastly different in temperament. They were studying in the 8th grade at a reputed school in Kerala. Anjaly was an average student, not exceptionally quick, but deeply committed and sincere. Aparna, on the hand, was the star of every class—bright, witty, and gifted with an extraordinary ability to grasp concepts in a snap.

But there was a secret flaw in Aparna's brilliance. She had a habit of postponing things. Homework, revisions, assignments—everything could wait until "tomorrow." She believed she worked best under pressure, relying on her sharp memory and intelligence to bail her out every time.

Anjaly was different. She knew her limits. She wasn't fast, but she was steady. While Aparna slept late and took things lightly, Anjaly would sit for hours, slowly piecing her lessons together, writing them down, revising them days before a test.

A Maths exam was announced. As always, Anjaly began preparing weeks in advance, practicing each problem again and again until her confidence grew. Aparna, confident as ever, declared, "I'll start the day before. No big deal."

But fate had its own plans.

On the morning of the exam, Aparna woke up with a high fever and a splitting headache. Her notes lay untouched. She stared blankly at her textbook, but nothing would stay in her mind. Panic gripped her.

Anjaly, though nervous, entered the exam hall with calmness in her heart. She had prepared for this. Aparna, on the other hand, sat frozen, unable to recall even the simplest formulas.

A week later, the results were announced.

Anjaly had passed—barely. Aparna had failed.

It was the first time ever.

Teachers were puzzled. "What happened, Aparna?" one of them asked.

She said nothing. But that evening, the silence broke between the sisters.

Aparna sat on the edge of her bed, tears threatening to spill.

"I messed up," she whispered.

"No," Anjaly replied gently. "You just got sick. That's all."

"No, it's not just that," Aparna admitted. "I've always postponed my studies, thinking I could manage everything in a night. I never really understood what I learned. You do."

Anjaly smiled. "That's because I know I can't memorize things in a day. I have to start early. It's how I work. You just have to understand how you work too."

Just then, their parents walked in. Sensing the mood, their mother sat beside them and said:

"Both of you are right in your own ways. But remember one thing—don't put things off for tomorrow thinking it will always be there. Tomorrow isn't promised. Do what you can today. That's all that matters."

Their father added, "It's not about being fast or slow. It's about knowing yourself. Your pace, your strength, your style. Measure your success by the effort you put in—not just the marks you get."

From that day on, something changed in Aparna. She still had her brilliance, but now she matched it with discipline. She stopped procrastinating. She started taking small steps every day—just like Anjaly. Not because she was afraid of failure, but because she learned to respect the value of today.

Moral of the story:

Stop procrastinating. Start understanding your strengths. Do what you can today—because today is yours, tomorrow may not be.

When the Forest Whispered Back

You were not born to meet everyone's expectations; you were born to live your truth, and let your silence be your strength.

— Ananya Roy

In a quiet village cradled between hills and rivers, there lived a wise Saint known for his silence, kindness, and insight. People from far and near traveled to seek his wisdom. But he rarely spoke—only when a heart was truly ready to listen.

One day, a young boy named Ishaan arrived at the Saint's ashram. His eyes were restless, his shoulders heavy with invisible burdens. He folded his hands and asked softly:

"Guruji… I try to be good. I help people. I do things with the best intentions. But still, I hear whispers. People blame me, judge me, and question my character. It hurts. I feel like nothing I do is enough. I don't want to argue. I just want peace… but I feel trapped. What should I do?"

The Saint looked at him calmly, then rose from his seat without a word. He gestured for Ishaan to follow.

They walked for a long time in silence until they reached the edge of a forest. Birds chirped gently, and the breeze rustled through a variety of trees—tall, short, leafy, thorny, flowering, and dry.

The Saint turned to Ishaan and asked, "What do you see?"

Ishaan looked around. "A beautiful forest, Guruji… full of different trees, plants, and colors."

The Saint smiled. "Can you imagine a forest with only one kind of tree? Just tall oaks, or only bamboo?"

"No," Ishaan replied quickly. "That wouldn't be a forest. It would be strange and dull."

The Saint nodded. "Exactly. The beauty of this forest lies in its diversity. In the same way, humans are not the same. Each person has their own personality, thoughts, values, and ways. Some will understand you. Some won't. Some will speak kindly. Others will hurt you—intentionally or not."

He paused, then continued gently, "You don't need to prove yourself to anyone. You were not born to meet everyone's expectations. If you spend your life trying to explain your goodness, you will lose the time meant for actually doing good. Keep your heart clear, your intentions kind. Even if the world closes its eyes, truth doesn't need witnesses. And those who truly matter—they'll see you, eventually."

Ishaan stood quietly, letting the Saint's words sink in like morning dew on leaves.

From that day on, Ishaan changed. He no longer waited for applause. He didn't stop to defend himself against every whisper. He smiled more, helped more, and lived with a lighter heart. And in time, those who had doubted him saw the quiet light he carried.

They came back, not to question—but to follow.

Moral of the story:

Stop wasting time trying to prove you're perfect. Do what is right and meaningful—people will recognize your worth when the time is right.

The Power of a Quiet Mind

Anyone can become angry — that is easy. But to be angry with the right person, to the right degree, at the right time, for the right purpose, and in the right way — that is not easy.
— *Aristotle*

Isaira, the only daughter of Vishwajeet and Sharvani, had just stepped into adulthood. At eighteen, she was bright, ambitious, and deeply emotional. But there was one thing that often overshadowed her goodness—her temper.

If someone disrespected her, even unintentionally, she would burst out in anger. Harsh words flew from her mouth before she could stop them. Sometimes, she exploded without any clear reason at all. And every time it happened, guilt followed. She cried silently afterward, overwhelmed by regret.

This emotional rollercoaster began affecting her deeply. Her parents watched her struggle, especially her father, Vishwajeet, who knew exactly what she was going through. He had been silently waiting—not to scold her, but for the right moment when her desire to change would come from within.

One evening, after another such outburst, Isaira approached him with tearful eyes.

"Papa," she said softly, "I want to change. I don't want to be this person anymore. It hurts… me and others too."

Her father smiled gently. "I was waiting for this moment, dear. Not because I wanted to point out your flaws, but because change is real only when we seek it ourselves."

He paused, then added, "Let me tell you something I've never shared before."

Isaira looked at him, surprised. "What is it?"

"I was just like you. In fact, I stayed that way till I was 40."

"Forty?!" she gasped.

He nodded. "Yes. I was rich, successful, and proud. I believed I had the right to speak however I wanted. I thought people feared me—and I enjoyed that. But I was blind. I was losing friends, trust, love. I was becoming… alone."

He continued, his voice calm, almost distant as he revisited his past.

"One day, after shouting at someone I loved, I saw fear in their eyes—not respect. That night, I sat alone and realized I had built walls around me. Not because the world was cruel—but because I didn't know how to manage my emotions."

"What did you do then?" Isaira asked.

"I read. I reflected. I found the root cause: I had allowed my emotions to control me. I started small—meditation, deep breathing, silence before reacting. I failed many times. But I never gave up. Slowly, I changed. And as I changed, so did the world around me. I regained the trust I had lost. I became calm—not because I had no fire inside me, but because I had learned when to let it burn, and when to keep it warm."

Isaira sat silently, taking in every word. She felt a shift inside her—not just inspiration, but hope.

"I want that too, Papa," she whispered. "Not for others, but for myself. I want peace… I want to grow."

From that day, she began her journey. It wasn't easy. But she stayed with it—one moment, one reaction at a time. She started journaling, practiced mindfulness, counted to ten when anger rose, and reminded herself of her father's words.

Weeks turned into months. And then, one day, she realized—she hadn't lost her temper in a long time. She had changed. Not into someone else, but into a better version of herself.

And with that, came happiness—not loud and showy, but quiet, deep, and lasting.

Moral of the story:

Don't let your emotions control your life. Master them, and you will master your peace. Short temper may speak loudly, but calmness echoes longer.

Beyond Grades: The Journey of Aarav

Everybody is a genius. But if you judge a fish by its ability to climb a tree, it will live its whole life believing that it is stupid.

-Albert Einstein

Aarav was a quiet 15-year-old boy studying at a prestigious school. Unlike his classmates, he wasn't interested in racing behind marks and ranks. Instead, he had a world of colors, lines, and dreams hidden in his heart — he loved to draw.

While other students filled their notebooks with formulas and essays, Aarav filled his last pages with sketches of the world around him. Unfortunately, his teachers didn't understand.

One afternoon, during a math class, Aarav was lost in his world again, sketching a lively picture of the classroom. The sharp voice of his teacher cut through the air.

"Aarav! What are you doing?"

Startled, Aarav stood up, his hands trembling. The teacher stormed over, snatched his notebook, and after a glance at the drawing, her voice grew harsher.

"Are you here to study or to become an artist?" she snapped. Without waiting for an answer, she sent him out of the classroom.

From that day, the situation worsened. Aarav's poor academic performance became the subject of whispers and angry glares. He often sat alone, carrying the weight of judgment he couldn't understand.

One evening, unable to bear it any longer, Aarav broke down in front of his father.

"Dad… I don't want to go to school anymore," he sobbed. "They only care about marks. They don't even try to see what I'm good at."

His father, Vishwajeet, listened patiently. He knew about Aarav's deep love for art, but he also understood the importance of facing struggles rather than escaping them.

Gently, he placed a hand on Aarav's shoulder.

"My dear boy," he began softly, "even the greatest like Bill Gates or Einstein didn't succeed by escaping challenges. They faced them in their own ways, patiently. Dropping out is not what made them great — it was their vision, their dedication, and their readiness to work harder than anyone else."

He continued, "Struggles are part of the journey. Don't run away from them. Grow through them. You have a gift, Aarav. But you also need the strength to face the world."

His father's words were like a spark in a dark room. Aarav wiped his tears and decided to try once more.

The next day, he walked into school with a new mindset. He began paying attention in class, completing his homework, and asking for help when needed. His progress was slow but steady.

Gradually, teachers who once criticized him began noticing the change. Aarav realized something deeper too — those who excel were treated with smiles and appreciation, but those who struggled were often left unnoticed. That realization carved a quiet promise in his heart: one day, he would make a difference.

Years passed. Aarav grew into a world-renowned artist and motivational speaker. When people asked him the secret behind his success, he always smiled and said,

"Talent is important. Hard work is important. But above all, kindness is important. Especially in schools. A teacher's role is not just to praise the toppers but to light the hidden lamps in every student. Don't judge. Understand. Support. Every child is a world of possibilities."

Moral of the story:

Treat everyone equally. Especially teachers — recognize that every child carries a different spark. It is not just marks that define them, but the dreams they dare to dream.

Keep Finding the Fragrance Within You

The wound is the place where the Light enters you.
— Rumi

Lakshmi was a bright teenage girl — sharp in her studies, quick with her answers, but often harsh in her words. Her aggressive tone, whether with friends or teachers, made her hard to approach. Despite her academic brilliance, people around her began to keep a distance.

One day, during a parent-teacher meeting, her mother visited the school. The teachers praised Lakshmi's marks, but their tone turned serious as they pointed out her aggressive behavior and her growing closeness with boys, which they felt was inappropriate. Her classmates too had started whispering about her.

Her mother was furious. On returning home, she scolded Lakshmi harshly.

"Are you going to school to study or to walk around with boys? I won't tolerate such behavior," she shouted, raising her hand on Lakshmi in anger.

Lakshmi was shattered.

Her father, who was working in Dubai, also heard of the incident and added to her scolding over a phone call. No one asked her side. No one asked what she was going through.

From that day, everything changed. Her mother withdrew warmth and treated her coldly. Her classmates avoided her. Her teachers didn't smile at her anymore. Lakshmi started feeling completely alone.

Ashamed and confused, she stopped talking to anyone. The only person who gave her a listening ear was a boy she had grown close to. He promised to stay with her and support her — but soon, even that relationship began to crumble.

Then, one day, their school organized a counseling session for students. The topic: Why teenagers should share their thoughts and feelings with their families. It was something Lakshmi didn't expect would shake her so deeply.

The Counselor Spoke to the Students:

"Till the age of 23, your brain is still under construction," he began gently.

"Your emotional decisions are stronger than logical ones. You may feel like you know everything — but you don't see the risks clearly yet."

He explained how the brain's decision-making center — the prefrontal cortex — matures only by the age of 23–25. Till then, emotions often overpower logic, making young people trust the wrong people or fall into unhealthy habits.

"That's why," he continued, "sharing with your parents or guardians is not weakness — it is strength. When you speak up, they can protect you from dangers you may not even see."

The hall was silent. Some students lowered their heads. Lakshmi's eyes welled up.

The counselor's words pierced her heart:

- "Your parents are not just there to control you, they are there to guide you."

- "If you hide your worries, you carry the burden alone. But if you speak, you may find someone willing to lift that weight."

- "Especially for girls — silence can be dangerous. If someone is manipulating you or making you uncomfortable, you must speak."

After the session, Lakshmi gathered the courage to speak to the counselor. Her voice trembled as she said,

"I don't have anyone... My mother doesn't listen. My father is far away. Everyone thinks I'm wrong. Please help me."

The counselor gently took her hand and said,

"You are not wrong, Lakshmi. You're just unheard."

He took her mother's number and scheduled a separate session with her.

In the Session with Lakshmi's Mother, the Counselor Shared:

"Your daughter is not a problem. She is a blooming flower that's been stepped on too early."

"Punishment without understanding creates wounds, not discipline."

He guided her through the importance of listening without judgment, talking openly about emotions, discussing body changes, teaching healthy boundaries, and being a role model.

"Children make mistakes. But they can be corrected with love, not fear. If you don't hear her, someone else will — and not everyone in this world has good intentions."

That day changed everything.

Lakshmi's mother returned home not as a critic, but as a listener. For the first time in a long while, she sat beside Lakshmi and asked,

"What's hurting you, Lakshmi? Talk to me."

Lakshmi burst into tears.

From then on, the mother became her support, her friend, her safe space. Slowly, Lakshmi bloomed again. Her studies improved. Her eyes sparkled with new hope. And her dreams grew big — she wanted to become a motivational speaker, to guide other girls who felt unheard like she once did.

Even though some teachers and friends never apologized, she decided to rise — for herself.

Moral of the story:

Each of us carries a fragrance — a unique, beautiful essence within. But sometimes, this scent is buried under misunderstandings, silence, and pain. The world may not always help you find your worth, but don't stop looking. Through every hardship, stay true to your goodness. Because when the time is right, even a crushed flower can bloom again — more fragrant than ever.

Awakening the Wings Within

You miss 100% of the shots you don't take.

— Wayne Gretzky

In a quiet village lived a teenage girl named Rahmath. She was known by everyone as a brilliant student — always among the top in her class, her head often buried in books. Her dream was clear: she wanted to become a teacher, someone who could shape young minds and guide them to a better future.

Rahmath was disciplined, focused, and determined when it came to her academics. But beneath that bright surface lay a silent struggle. She lived within the four walls of her comfort zone — never daring to step beyond. Making her own decisions terrified her. For every small or big issue, she turned to her family, seeking their guidance. Raised in a household where girls were expected to be obedient, quiet, and dependent, Rahmath grew up believing that important decisions were meant to be made by men. Her family had taught her to stay away from "outside matters," and to focus only on studies.

Because of this, Rahmath rarely interacted with her classmates. She spent most of her time in the library, nose buried in books, never pausing to ask a friend how they were or to share a laugh. She didn't know where most of her classmates came from or what they dreamed about. While others made memories, Rahmath lived in her silent bubble.

But life has its own way of teaching us lessons.

One day, a heated argument broke out between two boys in her class, quickly escalating into a physical fight. Chairs toppled, books scattered, and voices rose. When the principal heard about it, she called the students involved and looked for witnesses. The only person who had seen it all was Rahmath — but when the principal asked her to speak, Rahmath froze. Fear gripped her.

"I… I can't… I'm not supposed to get involved," she stammered.

She remembered her parents' strict instructions: *Stay away from trouble. Focus on yourself. Don't interfere in others' matters.*

So, she stayed silent.

Days later, something unexpected happened. Rahmath faced a serious issue of her own — a misunderstanding with another student that put her reputation at stake. To her surprise, none of her classmates stepped up for her. She realized with a sinking heart that her silence over the years had created walls between her and others.

That night, Rahmath lay awake in bed, restless. For the first time, she began to question herself. *Why do I feel so alone? Why doesn't anyone stand by me? Have I built this lonely world myself?*

The next day, she gathered her courage and approached her favorite teacher, Ms. Fathima, known for her kindness and wisdom.

With a trembling voice, Rahmath said, "Teacher… I'm so worried about my life. I have no real friends. My parents always told me to only study, not to interfere in anything else. But now… I feel lost."

Ms. Fathima gently smiled and placed a hand on Rahmath's shoulder. "My dear child," she said softly, "do you know when we truly become strong? Not when life is smooth, but when we face hardships head-on. Education is not just about grades and books — it's about shaping the heart, the mind, and the soul to survive and thrive in this world."

She paused, then began to tell a story:

"There was once a young eagle who lived in a nest on a high cliff. Its mother protected it fiercely, feeding it every day, and the eagle chick never had to move from its nest. One day, the mother eagle pushed the chick out of the nest. The chick panicked and flapped its wings wildly. For a moment, it felt as if it would crash to the ground — but then, something amazing happened. It discovered it could fly. The mother eagle knew that unless her chick was forced to leave its comfort zone, it would never learn to soar in the sky."

Rahmath listened, wide-eyed. Something inside her stirred — a realization, an awakening. She smiled faintly.

From that day on, Rahmath slowly began to change. She started greeting her classmates, offering help when someone needed it, and speaking up when she saw something unfair. She joined group discussions, made friends, and even volunteered in class activities. Her world expanded, and so did her confidence.

The girl who once believed she was meant only for silence and study became someone who could face the world with a brave heart. And in doing so, Rahmath didn't just become a better student — she became a stronger, wiser, and happier person.

Moral of the story:

True strength comes when we step out of our comfort zone. Education is not just about knowledge but about shaping the courage to face life. To live fully, we must learn to connect, care, and stand up — for ourselves and for others.

Madeena and the Mirror of Truth

The truth will set you free, but first it will make you miserable.

—James A. Garfield

Madeena was a bright and cheerful 13-year-old girl who wore the badge of goodness with pride. In school, she was known as polite, smart, and helpful. Her teachers praised her, and her parents believed she was an example of a model child. But behind her smile was a small secret — Madeena wasn't always truthful.

She had a habit of doing little wrong things — like taking colorful pens and pencils from her friends without asking and pretending they were hers. At home, when she forgot to do homework or broke a plate, she would make up small lies to escape scolding. But because she spoke sweetly and acted well in public, everyone thought she was a good girl. She thought, "No one knows the truth, so what's the harm?"

One day, something unexpected happened. Madeena wanted to impress her parents with high marks in the exams. When the progress report was given, she erased the real marks and wrote higher ones using a pen of the same color. She submitted the fake report to her parents and smiled as they hugged her and called her their "little star."

But the lie didn't last long. During a parent-teacher meeting, her class teacher showed the real report card. Her parents were shocked. Madeena stood there speechless, her head hanging low. For the first time, her mask had fallen.

When they returned home, her parents didn't shout. Her mother sat beside her and said, "We are not angry, dear. We are sad — because we trusted you." Her father added, "Telling lies may hide the truth for some time, but it never lets you grow in life. Let us tell you a story."

Her father continued, "Once in Japan, an old Emperor had no child and decided to find his successor. He gave a seed to every child in the kingdom and said, 'Whoever grows the best plant from this seed in a year will become the next Emperor.'

Children planted their seeds and brought beautiful flowers after a year. But one boy, Haruki, came with an empty pot. The Emperor asked, 'Why didn't your seed grow?'

Haruki replied, 'I gave it sunlight, water, and care. But it didn't sprout. I'm sorry.'

The Emperor smiled and announced, 'He shall be my successor! The seeds I gave were boiled and could never grow. All others replaced them. Only Haruki was honest.'

That one truth changed Haruki's life forever.

Madeena listened carefully. Her eyes welled up with tears. "So, if I keep lying, my growth will stop, just like the fake seeds?" she asked. Her father nodded gently.

From that day, Madeena changed. She returned the pens she had taken, confessed her lies, and promised to speak the truth — even if it was hard. Slowly, her teachers noticed the change. Her friends began to admire her honesty. Most importantly, Madeena started to respect herself.

Moral of the story:

Even a single lie can break trust and stop your growth. But truthfulness brings respect, strength, and a beautiful life. Be like Haruki — let truth bloom in your heart.